EXPLORING WORLD CULTURES

India

Kate Shoup

Cavendish
Square

New York

To Heidi and Olivier.

Published in 2016 by Cavendish Square Publishing, LLC
243 5th Avenue, Suite 136, New York, NY 10016

Website: cavendishsq.com

This publication represents the opinions and views of the author based on his or her personal experience, knowledge, and research. The information in this book serves as a general guide only. The author and publisher have used their best efforts in preparing this book and disclaim liability rising directly or indirectly from the use and application of this book.

CPSIA Compliance Information: Batch #WS15CSQ

All websites were available and accurate when this book was sent to press.

Library of Congress Cataloging-in-Publication Data

Shoup, Kate, 1972-
India / Kate Shoup.
pages cm. — (Exploring world cultures)
Includes bibliographical references and index.
ISBN 978-1-50260-580-1 (hardcover) ISBN 978-1-50260-579-5 (paperback) ISBN 978-1-50260-581-8 (ebook)
1. India—Juvenile literature. I. Title.
DS407.S54 2015
954—dc23

2014048020

Editorial Director: David McNamara
Editor: Kristen Susienka
Copy Editor: Cynthia Roby
Art Director: Jeffrey Talbot
Designer: Joseph Macri
Senior Production Manager: Jennifer Ryder-Talbot
Production Editor: Renni Johnson
Photo Research: J8 Media

The photographs in this book are used by permission and through the courtesy of: Sathish_Photography/Getty Images, cover; Uniquely India/Getty Images, 5; Tupungato/Shutterstock, 6; Aditya Singh/Getty Images, 7; Engraver G. Stodart based on painting by John W. Gordon, File:Marquis of Dalhousie.jpg/Wikimedia Commons, 8; Hulton Archive/Getty Images, 9; Mikadun/Shutterstock, 10; Indianstockimages/Shutterstock, 12; RBB/Getty Images, 13; Visuals Unlimited, Inc./Adam Jones/Getty Images, 15; Moment/Getty Images, 16; Muzlim/Getty Images, 19; Noah Seelam/AFP/Getty Images, 20; Alexey Makushin/Thinkstock, 21; Olaf Protze/LightRocket via Getty Images, 22; Gareth Cattermole/Getty Images, 25; Phil Walter/Getty Images, 27; Niels Busch/Getty Images, 29.

Printed in the United States of America

Contents

Introduction

India is a country in South Asia. It has lots of traditions, celebrations, and history. India is **diverse** because many different people live there. It is good to have different people and things in a country.

Different people ruled India for hundreds of years. Today, it is free. It is the world's largest **democracy**. It has one of the fastest-growing **economies** in the world. People from all over the world live and work there.

India is full of many beautiful places. It has mountains, rivers, deserts, and seashores. There are many colorful plants and beautiful tigers. It has more than two thousand **ethnic groups**.

Four big religions started there. More than 1,600 languages are spoken in India.

India is a special country to explore.

An Indian girl dresses in traditional clothing.

India is part of Asia. It is the seventh-biggest country in the world. It covers a lot of land—more than 1 million square miles (2.58 million square kilometers).

India is a big country.

The Ganges River is in India. It is very big. The Indian Ocean and the Laccadive Sea are to the south. The Arabian Sea is

India is a warm country. **Monsoons** bring rain to dry land.

to the southwest, and the Bay of Bengal is to the southeast.

There are eight mountain ranges in India. The Himalayan range has the tallest mountains in the world.

Bengal tigers live in India.

India has many types of animals. It has elephants, lions, tigers, rhinoceroses, and crocodiles. It also has forty-five thousand kinds of plants. Many of these plants are found only in India.

Endangered Species

Many types of Indian animals are **endangered**. To save them, they are put in parks and areas protected by the government.

People have lived in India for a long time. India began when the Indus Valley civilization settled there. It was one of the first civilizations on Earth. It lasted for two thousand years. After that, it broke into several parts. Each part had a leader. Some areas were run by foreigners.

The Marquess of Dalhousie was Governor-General of India from 1848 to 1856.

The East India Company started in 1600. It later handled half of all trading in the world.

In 1757, an English company called the East India Company bought land in India. Soon, England took over the country. In the 1800s, Queen Victoria became Empress of India. England controlled India until 1947.

In 1947, India became free. The first prime minister, Jawaharlal Nehru, was elected that year. He brought many good changes to India.

Father of India

Mahatma Gandhi (1869–1948) led India to freedom. The Indian people call him the father of their country.

Mahatma Gandhi

Government

India is the largest democracy in the world. It has twenty-nine states and seven territories.

Members of India's parliament meet in the parliament building.

India's government has three parts:

- Legislative: This part of the government is called parliament. People in parliament write new laws.

- Judicial: This part of the government is made up of the courts. It follows the Constitution. The

Constitution was signed in 1950. It describes the country's basic laws.

- Executive: The president and prime minister make up this part of the government.

Voting

All Indian citizens over eighteen years old can vote in elections.

India's parliament is divided into two houses. They are called the Rajya Sabha and the Lok Sabha. Parliament has 545 members. They gather in the Central Hall to pass laws. The Central Hall is in New Delhi, the nation's capital.

FACT!

The longest-serving prime minister of India was a woman named Indira Gandhi.

The Economy

For many years, lots of rules made it hard for Indians to trade with other countries. Now, India trades with countries all over the world. It trades mostly oil, coal, jewelry, and electronics. The economy in India is growing fast!

Indian rupees

The Poor

The economy is growing, but many poor people live in India. One out of every four people earns less than $1.25 per day. India is working hard to solve this problem.

Many Indians work as teachers, firemen, or policemen. Many others are farmers. They grow crops such as rice, wheat, cotton, and potatoes.

Indians also work in factories. They make clothes and machines.

Another important job in India is making movies. This industry is called Bollywood. It is located in Mumbai. Bollywood is the largest movie industry in the world.

Many Indians work on farms.

The Enviroment

People, plants, and animals need clean air and clean water to live. However, the air and water in India is dirty. Garbage is a big problem, too. We see this in large cities.

Unclean Air

In 2012, India's air was the dirtiest out of 132 countries.

Many Indians cook on stoves, called challahs. These stoves burn firewood and trash. This makes the air dirty. Smoke from cars and factories also hurt the air. The poor sewer system in India pollutes the water. Sewage is often dumped into rivers and lakes.

FACT!

More than one hundred Indian cities dump sewage into the Ganges River.

Many cities in India have dirty air.

Many Indian cities do not collect trash or recycle. That means there is a lot of garbage in India. This is very unclean. It also attracts bugs and rats. People in India are trying to clean up their country. This will take some time.

The People Today

More than 1.2 billion people live in India. It is the second most populated country in the world. Only China has more people.

India is a crowded country.

There are more than two thousand ethnic groups in India. These groups were formed in two areas of the country:

1. Indian families in the north.
2. Indian families in the south.

FACT!

One out of every six people on Earth live in India.

Staying in the Caste

Many Indian people marry others in their same caste.

Today many of these groups live and work together. Some are married and have families.

In the past, Indian people were put into five groups, or **castes**:

- Brahmins: Priests.
- Kshatriyas: Leaders or members of the military.
- Vaishyas: Farmers.
- Shudras: Servants for the other three castes.
- Dalits: Workers. They are considered impure and are very poor.

Today, a person's caste is less important. It is against the law to bully someone of a lower caste.

Lifestyle

Indian people have different ways of living. Nearly three-quarters of Indian people live in the countryside. These people live differently than people in big cities. Indians in the countryside live off the land. Many do not have electricity or running water. People who live in cities have a more modern lifestyle. They have computers, cell phones, TVs, and cars.

FACT!

Children in India respect people older than them. They are taught to never talk back to their parents or grandparents.

No matter where they live, Indians consider family important. Often, several family members live in one home. Sometimes, twenty people live in one house! Indian families are **patriarchal**. That means the men are in charge. However, Indian women have the same rights as men.

Many people living in Indian cities enjoy a modern lifestyle.

Marriage and Divorce

Most Indians have arranged marriages. That means their families choose their husbands and wives. Divorce is rare in India.

Religion

Religion is very important to Indian people. Four religions started there: Hinduism, Buddhism, Jainism, and Sikhism. Many Indians also follow Judaism, Zoroastrianism, Christianity, or Islam.

FACT!

Hindus do not eat beef. They see cows as sacred animals. In India, people who hurt or kill a cow are sent to jail.

In India, cows are sacred.

About 80 percent of Indians practice Hinduism. Hinduism has many traditions and rituals. Popular rituals include *puja* (worship), festivals, and **pilgrimages**. Some people call Hinduism the oldest religion in the world. However, no one knows exactly when it started.

The Taj Mahal

Even though most Indians are Hindus, India has no official religion. Everyone can believe in what they want.

People and Gods

Not all Hindus believe the same things. Some Hindus believe in one god, some believe in many gods, and some believe in no god.

Language

More than 1,600 languages are spoken in India. The most common language is Hindi.

Some street signs are written in both English and Hindi.

While many people speak Hindi, India has no national language. Instead, it has twenty-two "official languages." Hindi is the official language of the Indian government. In addition, each of India's twenty-nine states and seven territories has its own official language. These include languages such as Kashmiri, Nepali, Punjabi, and Urdu.

Some languages are called "classical" languages in India. That means the language is very old. Tamil, Sanskrit, Telugu, Kannada, Malayalam, and Odia are examples of classical Indian languages.

Hindi does not use the same letters as English. Instead, it uses something called the Devanagari writing system. It is very old. The words are written from left to right. There are no capital letters.

English in India

Many Indians also speak English. Often, they mix English words with Hindi words. When they do, it is called *Hindish*.

Arts and Festivals

Indians have enjoyed the arts for thousands of years. The arts include plays, movies, dancing, and singing. India has many beautiful sculptures and buildings. Many of these are very old.

Everyday Art

A lot of Indian art celebrates main religions in India. The most famous building in India, the Taj Mahal, is called "the jewel of Muslim art."

Indians enjoy watching movies and television shows. Indian music, theater, and dance are also popular. Indians also enjoy going to museums. The National Museum in New Delhi has more than 200,000 works of art.

FACT!

India's movie industry is called Bollywood. Each year, India makes more films than any other country.

Sonam Kapoor, a famous actress in India

Indians enjoy several festivals. One is called Diwali. It is a five-day festival to celebrate the new year. India also has three national holidays. Republic Day marks when the Constitution was accepted. Independence Day celebrates India's freedom. The festival Gandhi Jayanti honors Mahatma Gandhi.

Fun and Play

There are many sports to play in India. The most popular sport is cricket. It was invented in England in the 1500s. Cricket is like baseball. There is a bowler who pitches the ball, a batsman, and several fielders.

Men in Blue

The India National Cricket Team is nicknamed the "Men in Blue." This is because they wear blue uniforms.

The Indian people also enjoy several sports invented in India. One is *kho kho*. It is a game like tag. Another is *kabaddi*. It is also like tag, but you play it while holding your breath. A third is *pehlwani*, a kind of wrestling.

Virat Kohli is one of the "Men in Blue."

Playing in parks, visiting museums, or watching movies are other fun things to do.

Historians believe that chess was invented in India. Lately, it has become popular again. This is thanks to Viswanathan Anand. He has won the World Chess Championship five times.

Food

Indian people eat many different foods. The types of dishes cooked depend on what food is available. Popular meals include tandoori chicken, *rogan josh* (lamb), and *kaali daal* (lentils).

Favorite Foods

Rice and bread called naan are common in Indian dishes. Lentils and beans are also popular.

Indian dishes often have spices in them. Curry leaves are also used for cooking.

The foods some Indians eat depend on their religious beliefs. Many Hindus do not eat beef. They believe cows are sacred. Some people in other religious groups do not eat meat, fish, or eggs.

FACT!

Many Indian dishes have spices, but chilies are also common to use. They make meals spicier.

Indian cooking uses lots of spices.

Glossary

caste A hereditary group that defines a person's social status.

democracy A system of government in which leaders are chosen by the people.

diverse Differing from one another.

economy The process by which goods and services are produced, sold, and bought in a country or region.

endangered Describes when a type of animal is at risk of becoming extinct, or dying out.

ethnic groups Communities or populations made up of people who share a common cultural background or descent.

monsoon A seasonal wind that often brings rain.

patriarchal A word used to describe a system governed by men.

pilgrimage A journey to a special or holy place.

Find Out More

Books

Apte, Sunita. *India*. New York: Children's Press, 2009.

Sharma, Shalu. *India for Kids: Amazing Facts About India*. Seattle, WA: CreateSpace, 2013.

Websites

National Geographic: India

travel.nationalgeographic.com/travel/countries/india-guide

TIME for Kids Around the World: India

www.timeforkids.com/destination/india

Video

Mocomi Kids: India's Freedom Struggle

www.youtube.com/watch?v=cPjRaw8CVr8

Watch this video to learn more about India's struggle for independence.

Index

About the Author

Kate Shoup has written more than twenty-five books and has edited hundreds more. When not working, Kate, an IndyCar fanatic, loves to ski, read, and ride her motorcycle. She lives in Indianapolis with her husband, her daughter, and their dog. To learn more about Kate and her work, visit www.kateshoup.com.